Golden Arrows:

Poetry of Goddesses

Austie M. Baird
-Editor, Cover Artist-

Austie M. Baird is a born and raised Oregonian, holding both History and Education degrees from Eastern Oregon University. Long before becoming a wife and mother, Baird connected with the power of the written word, finding healing properties in both reading and writing. She draws strength from the beauty that surrounds her and the overwhelming love of her family.

A.B.Baird Publishing
Oregon, USA

Printed in the United States of America

First Printing, 2020

ISBN 978-1-949321-13-5

Cover Art Image by Austie M. Baird

A.B.Baird Publishing
66548 Highway 203
La Grande OR, 97850
USA

www.abbairdpublishing.com

Dedications

To Mom, Dad, Ben, and every kind soul who has ever taken a chance on me: thank you for believing in me, even at times when I didn't believe in myself.
-_Jessie Garber_

To my father; I did it.
To my mother, this is me.
To my brother, I am self-made.
To my sissy, you can be too.
-_Sundancer_

I would like to dedicate these poems to my daughters.
-_Sky Rose Heywood_

To all the women who rise above.
-_M.G.M._

For my daughters: Abigail, Moriah, Eliza-
with souls brighter than the sun, you are the future...
hold fast to your light, and remember to share.
-_Austie M. Baird_

For every woman who has ever been through something
-Nina Green

For my mom, dad, and brother, who were always there even when the words weren't.
-Iva Markicevic

To my daughter Aliza
and every woman around the world.
-Fahmida

To my family, friends and IG Poetry loves who believed in me when I didn't believe in myself, supported me and loved me for being me. Thank you for being in this journey with me.
-Phoebe Tee

Dearest Reader,

We wrote this book for you - because of what you've been through. We hope our words become a mirror to you: reflecting every emotion on the spectrum that comes with being a woman, in all of its power and glory. The storms, the mountain-moving, the elation, the rage, the passion, and... the purpose.

We wish that this book serve to remind you that you, you are brave. As you lift your head each day, ready to fight to become, refusing to settle for less than you deserve, giving fearlessly to others that light your house inside - we give you these words to inspire, to light that fire. By standing with and speaking up for each other, we continue the legacy that the women who came before us were brave enough to start.

We are the daughters of women warriors, troublemakers, queens who risked their reputations, freedom, and lives to build something better for us to inherit - traditions that we must continue; we owe it to our own daughters to leave behind a world in which they can dream.

We hope that you never stop feeling everything all at once, even when it would be easier to feel nothing. Because when you embrace vulnerability with courage, and feel and speak your truth, you empower those around you to do the same. This world is a big circus; what seems alluring is deceiving - but remember, you hold the master wand. There is nothing in this world that you can't achieve, nothing that is impossible, if you only believe in yourself.

We can help each other, straighten each other's crowns, wipe each other's tears - we can hold each other up when it gets tough. We can share the joy of our achievements. We can come together and carry on the work of those brave women who came before us.

We have come together to remind us all that we are not alone. We wish for you to take comfort in these words and most of all, show you that in here, with us, we will all always have a home.

And never forget:

You are always, without a doubt, stronger than you feel, wiser than you think, and more beautiful than you can see.

Table of Contents

<u>Iva Markicevic</u>

@sa.te.llights

Iva Markicevic is a road tripper, wave jumper, and amateur writer. Born in Serbia, she grew up in the United States and Canada, never settling in any one place for more than a few years. She writes to try to understand the concepts of place and home, to wage war against the inequalities growing up female perpetuates, and to connect with others who see language as the ultimate game-changer.

...why we write

it's sad but beautiful:

we write these words to build bridges,
provide connection, hope
for hurting souls
because we have walked the bridges
others wrote for us before.

-Iva Markicevic

...the world is heavier when we stand alone

we're seeing in indigo, and the world feels
a little colder now. it's like
the clouds cried, and no one paid heed,
so they left us the weight of their sadness
to teach a lesson that we don't seem
to be learning though we see
each others' shoulders stooping
under weights we never think to share.

-Iva Markicevic

… don't give them your wild

your wild scares them, little wolf.
they have not seen many
quite like you – fearless beauty
able to stand alone and
howl her own song.

i know they scare you, so you hide
in sheep's clothing
and seek out their approval, mistaking it
for love – love
is not something you'll get
from small men who'll only shoot you
should you take off your disguise.

you deserve better, little wolf.
shear off that sheep's wool, and bare your teeth.
you have a whole forest waiting for you
to claim it – do not neglect it
for a yellowing pasture
and a sea of barbed wire.

-*Iva Markicevic*

... she saw a different protagonist

that girl breathes fire
like the dragons from the fairytales
you used to read to her
when she was a child
in hopes of teaching her
blind obedience – that obedience
is exactly what she cheered against,
secretly preparing
for the day she would become a dragon
and burn the towers that you built down.

-Iva Markicevic

... wasting potential

how many astronauts are we losing
by raising our kids to believe
that only some of them deserve more
than the world they're used to?

-Iva Markicevic

... always trying to prove myself

i come undone,
unweave all the stitches
that made me whole
and let the thread fall to the ground
in the shape of a tangled galaxy.
from the inside,
i'm spilling apart
so that they see i burn bright.

they leave me
a black hole.

-Iva Markicevic

... math

the magazines told me
to let my boyfriend worry about math class,
that they'd teach me all the math
i'd ever need to know.
scales. tape measures. nutrition labels.
pounds. inches. calories.
subtraction. division. comparison.
less than. less than.

least.

-Iva Markicevic

... *dinner menu*

my first diet started
when i was 11. it had me
convinced that
puffed rice cereal and
strawberry yogurt
were an appropriate
dinner.
it taught me to
minimize
how much i need
because i thought i
didn't deserve
to take up space.

12 years later,
i stopped dieting,
started giving myself
permission
to take up the space
i need. still,
there are mornings i
look in the mirror
and reach
for the yogurt again.

-Iva Markicevic

... just breathe

i count – one, two, three,
four, five – to catch
my breath, to remind
myself these lungs still work –
and will continue to work –
even though it feels
like the rest of my body
is rallying against them.

-Iva Markicevic

... mother knows best

outside,
it's raining flower petals –

it's mother nature's hand offering
a box of tissues –

it's her voice saying,

"my child,
it's time
to wipe those tears away."

-Iva Markicevic

... *seeing clearer*

i used to misunderstand storm chasers;
i looked down on their choice
to be at the center of the
tornado, the hurricane. i already
housed the centers of the strongest ones
inside me, and all i wanted
was to run away, find shelter
that couldn't be blown away. i sit now
and watch a weather channel documentary
where the woman stands tall, eye to eye
with a devastating storm,
and for the first time in my life,
i see strength.

-Iva Markicevic

... it's never too late for a miracle

home is where the torn mittens are,
the ones i loved as a child
and refused to take off until that
sledding accident of 2005. i still have
the scar from it, on my hip,
and the mittens, reminders
that just for a few moments,
i flew, and the world looked magical.
it hasn't looked magical
for a few years now, but that unraveling yarn
makes me think it could, makes me think
i won't be too scared to soar
when the next miracle comes calling.

-Iva Markicevic

... *not the kind of love i want*

"it's a man's world,
and you've got to learn
to live in it."

(play by its rules
if you hope for
love)

but i don't call love
subservience, obedience,
and you wouldn't either
if it was you expected
to always put another's
needs before your own.

so i will learn
to love myself
in the ultimate act
of disobedience,
and little by little,
i'll turn
this man's world
into my own.

-Iva Markicevic

... *sweet tooth*

"you taste like sugar," he says against my lips.
i grimace. i never saw myself as sweet,
and i never want to. men with a sweet tooth
rarely respect who they view as candy,
girls they keep in little boxes and take out
to show off on the playground.
they never grew up, grew out
of boyhood tastes, never expanded
their palates beyond sugar.

-Iva Markicevic

... *compliments*

he tells me to lighten up,
to learn to take
a compliment.

but he's never had to walk down a street,
hearing strangers' unsolicited comments
about his tits, his legs, his ass.

if he had,
would he still think
i had compliments to accept?

-Iva Markicevic

... talking to a wall

"smile. sit pretty. speak soft
and slow. but only
when spoken to. else,
hush, hush, hush."

when i was born, the doctor told my mom
i had a good pair of lungs. when i was older,
my mom told me
i'd be a fool not to use them.

"don't be a bitch. calm down.
you're being hysterical.
you'd look better if you'd
smile, smile, smile."

you should say i'd ease your conscience –
isn't that what you're looking for
when even you must have heard
that oppression is wrong?

"i never..."

but you did, and you are. and
denials don't mean much
when actions speak volumes.

-Iva Markicevic

... know your worth

it took me a few years to comprehend
that this body is a temple,
but now that i have,
i will never again let in
anyone who treats it like a playground.

-Iva Markicevic

*... s** ed*

i say "sex" and am met
with shock, disappointed sighs.
but look at how, when i say "prince charming,"
their eyes open wide.
but i guess it's no surprise
when we've been waging war
on planned parenthoods
and using sex ed as a place
for girls to learn
to see duct tape as a symbol
for their self-worth –
*how lovely it is
we send our girls to school to learn
their bodies are objects
for men to own –*
how crass of me to say
there's something wrong
when there's a shortage of princes
and a ban on words,
when there's only one way
that this could go.

-Iva Markicevic

... one step forward, two steps back

there are days i look in the mirror and feel proud
of how far my body has come. how strong
it has become. but even on those days,
i reach for the pile of oversized sweaters
in my closet before i even think about
stepping foot outside.

(how long will it take me to learn
i'll never find self-love in others' eyes?)

-Iva Markicevic

... i stopped wasting my breath

it's the eyes, the hint
of a wall they betray,
that pull you in – you want
to save me by getting close,
skin to skin; you only focus
on the physical, visible.

but poison kills
even in small doses,
and i've been coating my lips
in venom since i was first told
i could put my mouth to better use
than talking.

(they never learn:
never get in bed with a scorpion
unless you have
an antidote.)

-Iva Markicevic

... careful

you wanted a koi pond
in a flawless garden
that i'm sure you imagined
i would tend to,

and you were right; i would,
but under my thumb,
it would grow into forest
with treetops that reach the sky
and give shade
to leaf-and-rock-studded
terrain, raging wild river
home to piranhas
with the sharpest teeth
and loosest judgment.

(be careful what you wish for.
it might just come back
and bite you.)

-Iva Markicevic

... a nautical tale

captain, dear, did you really think you could sail
your ship into my seas and i
wouldn't have anything to say about it?
you're mistaking me for the scared little girl
i once was. you'll find
it's much more difficult to manipulate
me now, now that i know i house
monsters within and control the winds.
this mist could easily become a storm
if you give me a reason.
are you afraid of lightning? you will be
once you see it illuminate
the graves being dug (on an island shore,
of course – you should have known
i never wanted you here), hear it whisper,
"this is for all the life
you took from her," see it come
for you and leave you in the dark.

-Iva Markicevic

... what i love most about myself

(i will never be one or the other)

daughter of two worlds
and two trains of thought,
i used to view home as
a sensitive topic
because there was no physical space
i felt i belonged, but this taught me
to mold myself into four walls
and an open door, a harbor for others
to find safety
when lightning strikes. i've become
the very thing
i thought i lacked, and that is exactly
what makes me strong.

-*Iva Markicevic*

... *vocabulary lessons*

i will teach my daughter
to say "no"
without guilt,
without explanation,
and to apologize
only for her wrongs,
never for her existence
or another's wounded ego.

-Iva Markicevic

... *sleeping is not a synonym for consenting*

maleficent and aurora work together now,
pricking the fingers of princes
who endanger all the kingdom's daughters
when they confuse saving
with taking advantage.

-Iva Markicevic

... the stronger bond

your name
is my name spelled backwards
in a language only we speak,
only we understand. we are
two pieces of a whole; we are
stronger together. your hands
lift me up, mend my wings,
keep me up when i can't stand.
they've tried
to turn us against us, but sister,
it will always be you
i choose in the end.

-Iva Markicevic

... you don't have to walk alone

call me on the afternoons when even your daydreams
feel like too much. i'll come and take
the weight you can't carry, set it on my back,
take your hand and follow
your lead as long as you need. i'll leave
when you decide
you need to walk alone, but until then, know
while this path may be yours alone,
the weight of its burdens doesn't have to be.

-Iva Markicevic

... herstory

your heritage is one of burial and pushing through
soil with the helping hands of the women
who came before you: the goddesses
who are often remembered as jealous
but rarely as brave; the queens
who bore the weight of their countries
alongside the skepticism
of the subjects they vowed to protect;
the visionaries who were burned at the stake as witches
then thrown into institutions all because they scared
a few weak men. your heritage
is a rich one, molded by mothers
who smile down on you, knowing you
will build the empire the bricks they left behind
were always meant to create.

-Iva Markicevic

Sundancer

@sundancer.poetry

Ra Anna Hoffman, aka Sundancer, is an alternative hippie alien whom works the Adult Industry by day and writes poetry by night. Taking inspiration from Leonardo Da Vinci, Sundancer has transformed herself into a true renaissance woman; an immensely talented artist with awards for photography and drawing before finding her voice in a more literal sense and tackling the medium of literature. This is her first publishing feature with hopes of releasing her own personal collection, "Birds of Paradise." When she is not reading or writing she is hiking the Central Coast, singing off key, making friends with every dog she comes across, and dancing in the street.

... 01/08/2020

We wait for recognition,
    lost in the too tall grass;
We begin to turn in circles
    chasing falling
        incandescence.
Why are we taught to be
undeserving of our own
        fragrance?

-Sundancer.poetry

... ordinary steps

Girls camouflage.
So many versions
of ourselves we can
choose to be.

In the most
ordinary of steps.

-Sundancer.poetry

... superstition

I live in a
ghost town
where intimacy
is as scarce as
gold and love
is a superstition.
I've been blessed
so I don't lose
my soul.
Playing with fire—
I shatter glass.
When I lose
I blame the ladder
but never the
black cat.
All this bad luck
stuck to my shoes
does nothing to
hinder this
gambling heart.

-Sundancer.poetry

... *fool for love*

I have always
dragged my feet
when it was time
to say goodbye.
I'm terrible at farewells,
when all signs
point to you
I ignored them all
for I am a
fool for love.

-Sundancer.poetry

... *supernova*

The horizon is full
of promise but the ground
has offered safety.
My eyes were always
drawn to my feet to
avoid looking at stranger's
backs as we emerge from
the earth with unbalanced
hearts and empty
stomachs.
Some have crashed and burned,
gone in a supernova explosion;
others cradled by the tide.
I want to go out
with my head held high.

-Sundancer.poetry

... *wild women*

We resonate with the
same frequency;
blood pounds war
and our hearts soften
the blow.
I fought the moon for standing,
wished on sailing rocks
for patience,
and listened to my
Father's sermon on
wild women.
They can only be tamed
with fire, he said
and every word from me
became an oath to praise
the next one's feet so
they know they were
not smothered but rather
lighter than air.

-Sundancer.poetry

... *dog food*

You ask for openness
so I split myself apart.
I cut my own heart from
it's safe haven and
placed it upon your altar.
Your final supper;
you feasted on it like a
desperate dog.
And even then, I
couldn't tell how hungry
I was until I noticed
your plate
was empty
and I
had nothing
to eat.

-Sundancer.poetry

... *propaganda*

I'm a flower girl.
I make love with
honest hands;
my propaganda promotes
a message
simply–
veritably,
when they earnestly
explore
your highlands
and lows.
There is no need
to read between
the lines
when I have summed
it up to a single word.

       – *Love.*

-Sundancer.poetry

... *inevitability*

I want them to call
me crazy. I want them
to see how I thrive
on these rolling waves
of life. Let them watch
as I float my hopes
on tiny paper ships
and open my palms
to inevitability.

-Sundancer.poetry

... formation

These soul birds
gather and chime,
twitter and bathe—
They sing me asleep
and I awake to
their call.
My morning,
glorious and illuminated
with their colors
and purpose;
we make love in formation,
we make love in formation.

-Sundancer.poetry

... do re mi fa so la ti do

I'll raise
    my voice
gracefully
      and
      gradually.

-Sundancer.poetry

... more than a feeling

There is this feeling
in my chest; I can't name
it, I can't name it
but it's bubbling,
bursting, burning a
hole in me
and I want it too.

-*Sundancer.poetry*

... infinite

We held hands since
the birth of us.
You taught me how
to dance to the sound
our love made,
and I,
like to think I showed
you how infinite
this dance can be.

-*Sundancer.poetry*

... *spring solidarity*

I'm made of water;
the lilies are my sisters.
We spring and bloom
in solidarity
and independence.

-Sundancer.poetry

... *peach*

I

looked at the view;
endless sea of glittering,

peach light.
A million lives below me,
a million
little victories.

-Sundancer.poetry

... labels

Graphite markings
on pristine pressed
white wood;
Hickory, Oak, and
rich Cherry,
we come from the
same forest
with the same need
to stretch our arms
towards the sky.
Labels redefined
with white wash—
we cry for
our existence,
smudged but not
erased.

-Sundancer.poetry

... 10.06.2018

I'm not the same.
I've shed skin;
    layer by layer
        to find the
    true essence
    of me.

-Sundancer.poetry

... 01.11.2018

I am not new to this
path of healing.
The sun is a familiar
sound of hope and
though I am inverted
at the moment I've
scratched wood along
the trail until
my soul was clear.
My ankles are weak,
busted from dog fights
in the bedroom,
so I was ruled by my feet.
Slow and steady, every
step I have taken has
been to reclaim my
faith in love.

-Sundancer.poetry

... 10.12.2018

I did it for love,
I did it for me.

-Sundancer.poetry

... survival of the fittest

When my winter bones
were picked clean,
spring blooms erupted
from the marrow
and dazzled the vultures.
They couldn't stomach
me then, so they
blocked out the sun
with figure eights.
My mistake was allowing
myself to wilt when I had
the moon to kiss my skin.
She knew my fears
and didn't hold them against
me but instead weaved a
path for my roots to follow.
There, the taste of deep earthed
water for my panhandling soul.
I've struck gold in the dark
all thanks to hungry pests.

Adapt to your surroundings, not to your haters.

-Sundancer.poetry

... get lost

My problem has
    always been
  I got lost
    in others.

This time around
  I'm going to get
    lost
  in myself.

-Sundancer.poetry

... primary colors

My skeletons
dance in the garden;
unashamed
of their nakedness,
the grass bows
to their presence.
They move by
design
and I admire
how they kiss
freewill
so fondly as their
primary goal.

-Sundancer.poetry

... ephemeral

An ephemeral flower,
    I'm trying to hang onto
    my gold
    and
through my growth
the seasons have
    taught me nothing
    is perfect
but every stage of me
    is beautiful.

-Sundancer.poetry

... miracle

I come alive
with every inhale
and with each exhale
I breathe a miracle.

-Sundancer.poetry

M.G.M.

@michelle.nicole.gerrard

Michelle Gerrard lives in Ojai, California. She is enchanted by the midnight sky. She wakes with dusk and rests with the sunrise. The water is another home. Animals some of her closest friends. She left pieces of her soul in Kenya, Australia and England. She yearns to feel all forms of love and to give love at every possible. She studied Creative Writing & Literature at Liverpool John Moores University and Loyola Marymount University.

... *flame*

Burning like a wildfire was all I knew how to do.
Passion.
Movement.
Bursting from the seams of my soul.
Time moved on, the fire
Burned,
Burned,
Burned, away.
Midnight stars ablaze. Flames cooling softly, slowly.
Everyday a desire for embers.
Teardrops from the sky.
A knowing that my fervor for life could still exist with
more profound strength if I learned to simmer the flames
within.
A glowing splinter smoldering in the ashes. Flickers of
golden light.

-M.G.M

... *a midnight melody*

A palpable loneliness lingered.
The quiet tumult of her soul in the land of milk and
honey
Where she waited in between the lines and dots,
The moon and stars.
The flowers sprang to fruition
Gleaming and withering
All int he dusky glow of midnight.

-M.G.M

... *trigger warning*

You pushed me against the wall, your hands too tight around my neck.

Your hands taking parts of me that weren't meant for you.

My body became a beacon of shame.

It could never be small enough.

Each rib I could see, became a reminder of the bruises that once covered the skin that housed them.

I became something of a ray of light.

A protective halo rose over me.

My eyes bright and blue, my skin iridescent against a darkened sky.

Purity could save me.

The hidden essence of my sexuality pushed into the same corner you backed me into.

There is an ember blooming within the depth of my being.

My body remembering what it is to sway and moan, to feel the cravings it always desired.

My breasts no longer bound, my obsession with the perception of virtue wilting, leaving, healing.

I was not born into this world to be placed on a pedestal.

Made into a porcelain doll you can carve yourself into.

I am a living, breathing being meant to occupy space, my body filled with longing desire, an insatiable appetite for more.

I no longer answer to those who marred my body.

I no longer succumb to shame.

I am whole. I am wanting. I am flesh and blood, so much more than withering bone.

A collision of fire and ice.

The feminine reborn.

-M.G.M

... more than flesh

The shedding of skin happens in the depth of shadow.

Leaving remnants of flesh behind.

The caverns of pain are endless. The gaping wounds a reminder of our fragile mortality.

We are more that flesh and bone. More than our physical pain. More than our shattering of pieces.

Even the gravest cut will heal.

So will you my love.

So will you.

-M.G.M

... in between dreams

Dreams are a strange place.

A parallel world within worlds.

Where touch becomes taste and sound becomes sight.
Our trembling waking bodies not knowing where reality
begins and dreaming ends.

I quietly yearn to stretch the night.

To stay curled up in the wonderland of dreams.
My body becoming song.

Vibrations through my skin, the fading of my eyes to dust.

Dust that dances, swirls, descending to the earth and lifting
to the stars.

My fingertips reaching to feel the evening, it's rapturous
fervor.

Here in the in between.

I am without being.

Am I flesh and bone? Or merely the stardust that makes up
the cells of a body that I am borrowing?

The blue in my eyes, is it really the particles of the ocean
that I drank while longing to become the strength of the
sea?

When I touch you, when I feel the softness of you against
me... do we become something else entirely?

A collision of time pausing.

The creation of memory that will linger on beyond the
waking of our dreams.

All as we dance between waking and slumber.
Somewhere in the ether.

Somewhere we are free.

-M.G.M

... the sway of a woman

The sheer strength of a woman can be found in her enduring heart, her undeniable fortitude, the quiet knowing of her mind, the fervent curiosity, effortless sensuality and mostly her uncanny ability to
Rise
From
The
Ashes.

-M.G.M

... *flower of the field*

When my life became moments of darkness I did not recognize. When I found solace in another's arms just to escape the reality of my every day.

My life sworn into black and white. The deepest depths of an endless ocean. The numbness of loss. A cavern black as night. I am drowning. Shallow edges deceive me. I feel your movements inside of me. I feel your heartbeat. Then in the blink of my tired eyes you are gone again.

From your once fluttering heartbeat I lost track of my own. A million facets of me floating into beams of light. Looking down upon my own devastated body.

Fetal position on a cold, damp floor. Covered in the saltiness of my own tears.

There is life yet, in this body and in this soul. Life to be created. Love to be given. And you, my flower of the field.
You broke me as much as you built me. And yet you were created in a time where my body had only known emptiness. The shattering of my being was a reminder that I was alive. That I could, despite all the loss create LIFE. That in despair, I could endure. You my darling child are the greatest teacher. The most beautiful reminder.

We are capable of rebirth. We are capable of being the most radiant bloom covered in scars, buried beneath layers of living. We are at the core...

Every shade of gray.

-M.G.M

... awake

Awakened.

The light seeped through the windows like golden
honey.

Dripping slowly, sweetly onto porcelain flesh.

The light found the scars, it illuminated them from
the shadows.

The desire to run back into the darkness ceased and
my body collapsed

Bathing in the warmth I had hidden from for my
whole existence.

-M.G.M

... *dream state*

Whispers of jasmine dance upon the breeze. You think you can define me. Cage me. A doll for you to hold. I have a universe inside me. Nebulas and falling stars. New planets forming and passing away.

Oceans flow through my veins, storms linger behind my eyes.

I will shatter the porcelain you see.

A million fragments like the stars that made me.

I am a dream upon a dream.

The way I love will leave you wondering if you are awake or sleeping.

Quiet now my darling, listen to my voice taking back what never belonged to you.

-M.G.M

... *in the orchard*

The Apple Orchard was cloaked in an ethereal mist.

The kind that wraps around your body leaving the smallest dew drops on your arms.

An intoxicating aroma of sweetness lingering on every inhale. The sun was still in hibernation, the sky speckled with purple and blue. The quiet broken by the sound of creatures coming alive and slowly stretching their sleeping bones.

Walking through these lines of trees will forever bring me back to the ephemeral moments of childhood wonder.

Times before my body knew what illness was.

Times before anxiety became a loyal companion.

Times before I had any concept of the fragility of life.

A time when time itself had no bearing on my life.

When the smallest trinket was the greatest pleasure.

When I measured my days by the amount of laughter, the pinecones and berries in my basket, the sticky sweetness of apples on my lips.

In the midst of the chaos and enduring hardships of adulthood, a body that ails, forever goodbyes and the grief that accompanies them... I go back to the orchard. Sometimes I lie on the cold, wet Earth.

I stare upward to the dark clouds and twinkling stars then watch them fade into the orange blossom of sunset.

I tell myself that in this singular moment all is well. This inhale and exhale mean I am still here. I can still love.

I can still feel the blood coursing through my body.

I am reminded that I am somebody's Harvest and they are mine. And even when it comes time to leave this Earth... that simple fact will be enough to hold me across all the cosmos. And so we burn in magnificent flames and fade into embers all in a field of magnificent life

-M.G.M

... *contradiction*

And if I could describe exactly what my soul feels like it
would be:

The ocean and the forest colliding.
A contradiction.
A meeting of two not like the other.
Chaos
Fury
Black holes
Of depth that have yet to be understood.
Calm
A place of pulsating life.
Sturdy.
Enduring.
Movement and stillness all in one breath.

-M.G.M

... *worth*

The fragility of a butterfly soul.

The delicacy of the hollow bones of a hummingbird.

The dark between the stars.

My darling, you are made of a whispered grace.

A silent courage that needs not roar.

Your body moves as though it is blooming with the way you reach for the ever open sky.

A voice that belongs to the mythological goddesses.

The sirens who sweetly called their lovers into a sea of pleasure and death.

My sweet child, please know:

Just because he doesn't see you
Just because he doesn't want you
Doesn't mean you aren't worth fighting for.
Your worth is not determined by another.

The very beating of your heart
Is all you ever need to reach for when the words, "I'll never be enough" fall out into the universe.

You are enough. You are more than anyone could ever dream.

-M.G.M

... *stillness*

Flaxen fields unmoving in the heavy humidity of dusk.

The only sounds are the whimpers of coyotes, the sigh of the trees, the chattering of owls.

My skin feels less my own.

More of the stars.

Kissed by citrus pollen.

There is a rhythm in stillness.

A steady beating of drums.

A reminder of our impermanence, a testament to how we belong to nature above all else.

Our toes should be buried in the Earth, our hair windblown with petals laced into every strand.

Our lips as sweet as honeysuckle.

Our fingertips smelling of wild jasmine.

Our eyes beaming with the light of the moon.

There is nothing more than this right here. This is enough. This is everything.

Be still

-M.G.M

... golden light

Love has a way of wilting or blooming,
When your eyes begin to flutter.
The nature of loving,
Is freedom.
It's defiance that is as strong as it is delicate.
It does not rest in the light or dark.
It makes a home somewhere in between.
Love, smells of lemongrass after a tropical rain.
Intoxicating. Seductive. Yet Familiar.
Love will always bring pain.
You will have wounds deeper than the black holes
Lurking in the depth of the seas we have yet to
explore.
But they will make you glow with life in
remembrance of how they came to be.
You will love many hearts.
You will become woven into countless souls.
Let it all in.
Take the wounds.
Nourish them with your tears.
Become love.
A radiant beam of perplexing light that never ceases
to shine.
Even when the darkness falls.
You are the golden beam of sunset.
The sleeping dandelion.
The kiss of lightning during a thunderstorm.
You are love.

-M.G.M

... trace

We are the feral beasts of the tender estuaries
Atop an eternal vista where the sea below
Lures us into her cascading waves
Like the ancient creatures we once were
Bringing our connection back to life.

-M.G.M

... bloom

Kaleidoscope of radiant color.
She is the reflection of light, the flash at the edge of
the horizon.
The way she rises at the dawn makes even the sun
envious of her warmth.
Happiness blooms within as you fall even deeper in
love with her enigmatic, fractured soul.

-M.G.M

... painting

She was created to be painted. Every curve and edge to be explored.

Calendula laced, sun kissed skin. Lashes touched with dandelion blossoms.

Scars that become kisses strewn across a blank canvas. Her soul only half complete.

Begging for color, burning covet for touch.

Broken and whole.

Broken and whole.

A painting yet to be imagined.

-M.G.M

... roots

She was made of wild things.

Hair that never settled, flying upward with the slightest breeze.

Eyes that darted here and there, never settling on one focal point.

She was a rider of the wind, sailor of the seas. Roots were a foreign thought.

An elusive concept placing oneself in the ground, the commitment of staying in one place to grow.

Terrifying and yet oddly desired.

Balance.

Find a way to ride the wind and bury oneself all at once.

Earth and air intertwined into a world of luster.

-M.G.M

... *la luna*

You know when the moon is at her fullest and her light streams down on the ocean like one million stars cascading from the night sky?

A thousand kisses to calm the chaotic beauty of the sea.

She is the very chaos.

The passion, the love and the tenderness.

If you look close enough you will see her smile

Striking and endearing

Shining back at you.

-M.G.M

... by night

The arch of her foot and the curves and edges of her
waist.

The mahogany scar on her shoulder met by the steady
gaze of ocean eyes that tell a story with every piece
of light that radiated off them.

By night one discovers the details of human flesh
illuminated by the moon, the stars, headlight, and the
reflection of a midnight sky on a raging sea.

Details that get lost in the stark light of day.

The kiss on the side of her mouth when she smiles.
The freckle on the tip of her nose.

I remember from touch more than sight. By the sound
of her voice more than the movement of her lips. The
aroma of rosemary from her hair...lingering still.

How well we loved...myself and I in the shrouded
cover of nightfall.

-M.G.M

... why

Tell me why everything must die.

Each blossom only here for a flicker of time.

Every day of living bringing us closer to an end. Or is it a new beginning? The greatest adventure we have yet to know?

Why does music seep into our souls... the melodies so familiar? A million questions with no real answers. Perceptions. Ideas. Religions. Science. A flower to one is a weed to another.

Isn't there peace in that very knowledge?

That our heartbeats can align but our minds never will.

That the world will always be filled with an endless amount of questions and an even more endless amount of answers?

I don't believe we should ever stop asking why or searching for purpose in this existence... but we should take a moment and smile.

We will never know or see every answer. Just maybe we will become the answer. Some day in some place on some star. We will become.

-M.G.M

... *emerald bay*

Clouds shatter to reveal rays of sunlight

They fall through the pines

Illuminating the settled snow below.

Tiny ice crystals gather and dance on the radiating light.

I run my hands through the diamond dust

Memories of you flooding my soul.

Essence.

Pine melts into springs honeysuckles.

The emerald waters so like your eyes, an uncanny blue with hidden forest green rivers throughout.

The snowflakes fall and I remember your fingers as they traced the outline of my being.

As we walked in the mist, the cold engulfed us and yet we noticed nothing but one another's warmth.

It was here in the majesty of nature that I knew it would forever be you.

Constantly.

Continually.

Consistently.

You.

-M.G.M

... *spring*

She speaks in flowers.

I remember flowing cotton fabric, the smell of cilantro, doe brown eyes that always met mine with love.

The smell of eucalyptus on his skin. Lips that I had felt like I had known before, in another time, another life.

I remember the soft flesh of avocado speckled with pink salt crystals.

The way the sun lured out the green in his eyes, the sweet sound of wind through tall trees.

Hands tracing the edges of my face, memorizing the stars in my soul.

Defeated. Rejected. Scared. Alone.

Silence and his arms around my waist pulling me close and his voice saying... stay here with me.

I remember bits and pieces, fragments of whole photographs.

The painful moments blend gently like watercolor into the beautiful moments.

At times they all come flooding through my being and it is almost if I am made entirely of memories.

Bittersweet thoughts.

We will one day be nothing but a memory.

Our flesh, our breath will no longer be of this world.

One day our smell, our hair, the vibrancy of our eyes will only be engrained in the minds of those who experienced our living being.

In the same breadth, a privilege to be remembered.

And just as flowers bloom, we bloom and just as they wither, we wither.

Just as there is astounding beauty in blooming, there too exists extraordinary, breathtaking beauty in fading, in leaving this world just as we came into it.

-M.G.M

... the gift of age

Lemon myrtle whispers on dew kisses skin. The heaviness of the sun ripened mango resting on the still air. As time moves fluidly, an ever flowing river, the flesh shifts, wilts and breathes new life.

Paint strokes around the eyes. Touches of silver in auburn hair. Fragmented pieces of a broken heart finding peace within an aging body.

Only when this temporary vessel starts to languish do we begin to understand the enduring nature of the soul. How the child like wonder can be found buried behind glittering eyes.

How flesh and bone are merely an illusion that our true selves is borrowing, playing, experiencing.

When we look into faces we should see beating hearts and smiles that light a room with their grace. When we see laugh lines and hands hardened from labor and lives many burdens we should see stories, possibilities and the extraordinary beauty that exists in every imperfection.

Not all of us get to see our first silver locks. Too many come into this world flickering and they burn out before they even experience their first words. Not knowing the feeling of a lovers touch or what sheer heartbreaking awe you are left in when you love a child.

Too many will never see tomorrow and so we find gratitude in our own mortality. Find solace in the lack of knowing when we will leave this place. Find hope in the rhythm of the present. The gift of age may be the most incredible honor bestowed on anyone. Youth is divine but age means you have been granted the chance of life.

Live it dear one.

-M.G.M

... summer

Vibrant.

Bold.

Soft.

Rich.

The morning skies alight with a rusted orange glow.

The afternoons a silent blistering blue.

The evenings water colored with periwinkle, lavender and rose.

People floating under the stars. People filled with ever changing pallets.

Desire. Anger. Frustration. Joy. Curiosity. All omitting waves of pulsating color.

The warmth of few drops settling on the skin. The simple painting of a Summer Dawn.

-M.G.M

... *shine*

Stars have never needed anything other than themselves
to shine.

They create their own light.

Dying just to have the chance to kiss your skin.

Settling like the morning dew.

-M.G.M

... *grow*

The crisp winds of winter fall into the pulsating growth of spring.

Summer comes with the piercing heat. Heat that suffocates and inspires nostalgia for youth and long forgotten love.

Autumn. Sweet Autumn. A time often seen as the beginning of death. And yet look at the abundance of colors, the rosiness of women's cheeks, the romance of cinnamon and nutmeg sprinkled on the breeze.

The seasons remind us that our live is constantly in transition. Moving. Ebbing. Flowing.

The desire to stay still. To stand in a moment and relive a smile, a feeling, a gentle touch. It calls us deeply. Stay. Stay here and do not let time consume you.

But we cannot stay. Even when we want to. Even when it means letting go of people and places we love so dearly.

We must allow our roots to become unhinged. The wind to carry us. The caressing of new earth, the hands of new love, the sound of new voices.

We are capable of so much more than we will ever know. Capable of greatness within adversity. Caple of enduring the gravest pain.

When you forget your own ability to move forward. Look to the seasons. The way they come and go. Seamlessly allowing themselves to change. Year after year. Day after day.

Falling in love with the transition.

-M.G.M

Nina Green

@nina_green_poetry

Nina Green is a poet from the UK. She writes mostly about the ordeals, inconveniences and unacknowledged triumphs of being a human, and occasionally hides secret messages in her poems. She finds endless inspiration from the way we each weave unique narratives from experiences that can never fully be explained. She feels most at home in a city or by the ocean, and is a collector of books, coffee mugs and unusual things from strange places.

... church of ash

Perhaps I am just a mourning moon
casting light over a paper town
that you crushed between your desire and your fear.
Or am I a dead poet,
scribbling nonsense in newspaper margins
and twisting the reality of love
into a middle-of-the-night daydream?
I think you just pretend to be lost
because it sounds braver than hiding.
Or perhaps you really are just a fool,
in love with a Russian doll
who's playing mind games
while your house burns down.
Either way,
we will both scar
and if we ever say our vows,
it will be within a church of ash.

-*Nina Green*

... *burnt wings*

You skipped town when the rain fell,
while I watched continents rearrange around me,
and I realised I lost someone who was never really mine.
I always did shine brighter than the sun, and how could
you resist that?
The crimson phoenix who learnt to fly on burnt wings.

It was no excuse to set her sky on fire and walk away.

You were a small man, hiding behind your suburban
mask.
Masked men have no real courage, only entitled curiosity.
And when you realise you're in too deep
(when you realise being a real man isn't taking the easy
option)
you crumble like a child.
And that is how you lose the phoenix in the sky,
who burns brighter than the sun.

-Nina Green

... *thank you*

You watched my heart rot away
while I waited for you to say you love me.

You put me in a cage much too small
and pretended you didn't have a key.

You told me I had a beautiful soul
as you tried to take away its sparkle.

And I would say thank you,
but you'd never understand what it was for.

-*Nina Green*

... *battleground*

I am just a sculpture,
formed in the violent hands
of a monster pretending to be a husband.
I am just a product of a war
waged in the mind of a little boy pretending to be a
man.
I am hardened like the earth beneath the soldier's feet.
Barren like the battleground.

A creation born of ignorance;
"a war on women will make men stronger."
I am just a product of a war that was never mine.

But so were the poppy fields.

-*Nina Green*

... annie

You've been calm in the face of chaos
and kind in the face of the vicious.
You've healed the unhealable and walked the unwalkable.
You have been protector, leader, counsellor and child.
You've fought battles you've never talked of
and suffered wounds you've never complained of.
You are fierce and soft and fire and water.
You are mother and friend and lover and daughter.
You are human.
You are woman.

-Nina Green

... the garden

I watch you die and come back to life over and over
again.
I watch you weather storms and frosts in quiet resilience.
And I watch you open and bloom in the sunshine as if
winter does not exist.
And then I remember that I am also a creature of this
earth,
and I can do the same.

-Nina Green

... *heartbeats*

I'm certain that when the trees rustle,
they are whispering "be strong".
And I'm certain that when the wild river gushes,
it is shouting "be free".
And I am certain that when my heart beats,
it means to say "you are worth more".

-*Nina Green*

... *paper moon*

I used to have this crazy idea that I was bullet proof;
invincible.
But you climb inside my skin and I go up in flames like
a paper moon.

But it isn't wise to not notice the salted laughter of the
mistress who keeps your secrets.
Even the most fragile (strong) women have battleships
hidden in their waters.
I am white petals, full of hope and easily crushed.
But I am also raven's eyes and black clouds and salt in
your wounds.
Do you know a praying mantis eats her mate once she's
done with him?
You taught me that I'm not bulletproof, and I'll teach you
that I'm not just a paper moon.

-*Nina Green*

... *feelings exist for a reason*

I will wear my sadness like sunglasses and my anger
will be my sunhat
and you will take me as I am or not at all.

-*Nina Green*

... *place of refuge*

Sometimes I'll go out of my way to step on an extra-
crunchy-looking dried leaf.
Sometimes I smile at the morning mist because I get
to start my day walking through the clouds.
Sometimes I'm just grateful for coffee and yellow
dahlias and squishy pillows and the sound of your
voice.
Sometimes my eyes are wide open to the way that
every single moment is enough.

And sometimes I swallow so many "needs" and "not
enoughs" that my belly aches and my heartstrings
snap and I drown in thoughts of all the lives that
could have been and all the truths I never said and all
the ways that life has disappointed me with cages and
glass ceilings and empty promises.

So, my place of refuge is those micro-moments that
have flowers and coffee and crunchy-looking leaves.

-*Nina Green*

... *freedom*

I have learnt that freedom is earnt from being burnt.
A phoenix; red feathered and flooded with fire.
Like air I rise.
Like smoke on a frozen morning.
Dropping shards of broken pasts.
Breathing dreams of a thousand futures.
Blind to the path.
But running anyway.

-Nina Green

... *woman*

By body has been ripped open
in wars you will never comprehend.

My mind has walked through worlds
that most men would run from.

And my heart has loved harder than most ever will.

I am not a woman for weak souls, shy feelings or frail
boys.

-Nina Green

... zen

I sat on the edge of that cliff and listened to the voice
of the ocean,

and when she cried it was no less beautiful than the
moon that keeps me up at night.

So this is my letter to you; to my ocean and my moon;
my church and my home.

Even when all seems lost, when the future is dark and
life is pointless and lonely,

I look at you and I see the meaning, I find the
important, I reach zen, if only for a little while.

-Nina Green

... dear daughter

Dear daughter,

I'd like to tell you that you don't need to change for anyone.

But changing for other people gave me the skills to change for myself.

And I'd like to tell you to never ever slack off at school.

But slacking off taught me the value in hard work.

And I want to tell you to stay well away
from the boys who will try to push your boundaries.

But it is those boys who taught me that boundaries matter.

And I want to tell you to stay away from those pretty girls
who bitch about people behind their backs.

But it's those girls who taught me that kindness is the real beauty.

And I wish I could make you stay away from people who don't care about you.

But it is those people who taught me to care about myself.

Dear daughter,

I wish I could keep you safe.

But safety never taught anyone anything.

-Nina Green

... how to choose a guy.

Does he respect you? Your soul, your body, your opinions, your growth, your sparkle? Can he value your inner world and does he show you the wonders of the outer world? Does he have a thirst for knowledge? A desire to learn about who you are and who this vast beautiful universe is? Will he fight for you with the fierceness of a mother wolf protecting her cubs? And will he care for you with equal softness? Does he see what is underneath your skin and will he show you who he really is; the vulnerable parts, the bits he hates, the ugly sides? And will he look upon those same parts of you with compassion or distain? Can he exist without others? Does he enjoy his own company and can he give you space to enjoy yours? Can you talk? Really talk. About life and philosophies and politics and handbags and boot polish and bathroom tiles and how beautiful the trees look? Can you laugh together? Can you laugh until tears run down your faces and your bellies ache with it? And can he laugh at himself as well as this dark world? Can he forgive without judgement or grudges? Can he get excited with all the joy of a child? And can he be serious when it is called for? Can he be your best friend, your brother, your husband and your fling?

And if he can't, can you be brave enough to walk away?

-Nina Green

... cake is good for your soul

Promise me you'll remember that it's okay to let those
tears leak.

That the days you can't get out of bed make you tired,
not weak.

Promise me you'll remember that you have it in you to
be all the things you think you're not.

You can be courageous and kind and determined and
everything else that you forgot.

Promise me you'll remember that humans make mistakes

They screw up, freak out and eat way too much cake.

Promise me you'll remember that your anger is there to
protect you from the pain.

And everyone feels like they're going insane.

We're all fighting battles, and no one feels that tough.

Promise me you'll remember that you are good enough.

-Nina Green

... men

Learn the difference between a good man making a few bad decisions,

and a bad man making a few good ones.
It's important.

-Nina Green

... you are worth more

You are worth more than to be missed
only when he is lonely.

You are worth more than drunk texts at ungodly hours.

You are worth more than a quick coffee while he is on
his way to somewhere else.

If he sees you only as an option, do not give him the
choice.

-Nina Green

... leaving

If you ever stand in front of him; not knowing if you
should stay or go,
and he doesn't wrap his arms around you...
leave.
And don't you dare go back.

-Nina Green

... libraries

Are you really so resolute in your fear of being alone,
that you would cling to what you don't deserve?

A suffocating comfort zone
that continues to shrink you into
a tiny scrap of what you could be.

You have traded your soul for a man
of muted colours and filtered dreams.

We are all living stories.

When some people just want to be postcards,
go be an entire library.

-Nina Green

... *i sit and i listen*

I sit and I listen
while you tell me you want to hurt yourself.
You want to cut the skin from your vagina
and the tongue from your mouth.
All the places he touched you.
Skin them away.

I know you won't.
I know your strength.

But I know your mind
is playing those images
over
and over
and over
and all I can do is pray
that you also see me too,
standing here,
loving you.

-*Nina Green*

... *breathing*

Breathe.
Breathe through the pain.
And the despair.
And the fear.
Breathe until you remember who you are.

-Nina Green

... *remember*

In this battle,
remember whose side you're on.
Remember love,
remember peace,
remember who you are.

Everything comes to an end.

And sometimes we leave pieces of ourselves behind
because we forgot to be on our own side.

-Nina Green

Jessie Garber

@cosmic.ramblings

Jessie Garber is a 27-year-old writer and native of the south Chicago suburbs, who lives in Virginia with her fiancé and their two rescue dogs. She holds a B.A. in English and political science from Illinois State University and is currently working on her master's degree at Georgetown University. Jessie wrote her first short story at age six and formed an early love for poetry, which was enhanced upon finding a second-hand copy of a Robert Frost compilation. She believes poetry, at its core, is an ode to small moments, like the way the light shines through the trees and how gumption feels at the pit of our stomach when we decide to become who we were always meant to be. Jessie is also the author of a 2017 children's book titled 'A Day in the Life of Madam President.'

... brave enough

when listless calls
we stitch wings to our heels
and let the wind carry us
to our latest soul sanctuary
molding vision into memory
swirling dreams in our cups
until the mundane feels extraordinary
like it did before upward growth made
home feel elusive as the sand at our feet

so we sit and watch
the ocean glint gold, let sea foam paint us
in lust for adventure and *please-love-me-holy's*
but when sun settles we drink moonlight like tonic
basking in the fact that we were brave enough
to trade comfort for an endless chase:
the insatiable wild
within us.

-*Jessie Garber*

... *awestruck*

i'd scour the earth
to find the kind of *a l i v e* that
lives in mountaintop views
and leaps from planes at 14,000 feet
—i've made those journeys, elated
as my hand grazed perpetuity
but i still have never known *awestruck*
the way that i do when i notice
just how delicately the light
shines through the trees.

-*Jessie Garber*

... *ribs*

i used to think
that strength meant *speak*
until i felt *l i s t e n* calling
to me, so i op e n e d
my ears and closed
my eyes, felt the universe
wrap-'round-my-ribs
like holiday lights
and in the glow
and the warmth it
whispered to me true;
the answer, in my bones
i already knew.

-*Jessie Garber*

... *murals*

train your heart to hear the quiet
through the clatter. to know that not
all things that can flash should. do them
anyway. silently. let the storms that circle
inside your chest make murals of its walls.
let them swell and wedge mountains between
moments and what we care to speak of
them. not all thunder was borne to saturate
pages in rain. sometimes the echo was
meant to change us. honor it. and know.
you must keep some things for yourself.

-Jessie Garber

... *glisten*

i find the words each time
i watch the sun glisten

on the river; bewitched by
golden gleam that moves my

soul to speak, but only once the
universe knows i am listening

—*it's then i can hear the poetry*

-Jessie Garber

... *peeling*

the rind of the years is
rough, but when peeled
back so much sweetness
d r i p s. slow like

forgetting, but time, still patiently
impatient in its passage. it st ains
our fingers with r u by, meanwhile
our hearts carry the f
                            all
                                    ing seeds

            that litter our floors.
we start anew. after the boiling,
the days m e lt from memory
but upon cooling, all that
remains is the feeling;

always the coming home.

-Jessie Garber

... *longing*

for years i waited for
loud to satiate the honeyed
longing at the bottom of
my stomach(it had sunken
like a wooden ship)

i drowned it with *busy* but
still, it would not be quelled by
the noise or the lights or ego's
whisper to me(*you need this
and you need that too*)

but today, as i opened the window
and felt the cool breeze trace my skin, i
looked outside, m e s m o r i z e d
by the leaves

and i felt it.

you see, they were falling like
crumpled pie c e s of torn-out pages
from stories i no longer tell and
i thought,

how much *p e a c e* there is
in tearing out the chapters that
do. not. define. me. and simply
watching them

      l   *a*
f   *o*   *t*   *away.*

-Jessie Garber

... saccharine

i have always tasted
saccharine promise in
autumn's return, for
the crumpled leaves
cascading from branch
through apricot sun
taught me that
we too can shed
all things outgrown
and still be
born. again.

-Jessie Garber

... dusk

i have hung low in
setting skies, seen my
peachy-keen clouds muddled
by the ruddy dark of night, but
before dusk devoured my will, i
saw it conjure a final neon flare(it
was coral and vermilion and
orchid—i wish you could see
how *br i g h t)*

it's true that *g r a v i t y*
may magnetize my feet to the
dirt and the earth, but
in this one last fleeting burst
is reverence to tomorrow, so
as the colors fade and i inhale
the thick of defeat(to lower and rest,
and rest and repeat)i know
i will rise again
tomorrow.

       l   l rise.
     i
i   w

-Jessie Garber

... *wild indigo*

where do i go when i go
i'm turning
into a falling star
burning through kitchens
coveting the blood moon
with twilight kisses i am
searing pages of plans
to sail belly-up in the cool stream
finally, i am seeing
bruised fruit for parts still
useable, i am slicing open
and peeling or rather
time has peeled me but
either way i am blazing through
wild indigo faster and farther
than ever before
now that i am no longer
afraid
of gravity.

-Jessie Garber

... to become

i see a bluebird on my way
into work and i want to tell you that
i wish i could say it will all be easy.
wish i could shake the hands of all the
passersby and promise them the same.
but sometimes there are bouts of insomnia
from glorious, incorrigible wonder and
tired eyes that sparkle over sunlit coffee
and citrus juice. what i *have* to tell you is that
this sun will rise again until it doesn't.
mostly, i should tell you that all we can do
is give and give and give again until we are
aching with grief or bursting with joy.
it's this either-or that is life's boundless gamble
but it is the worthiest one; for it is only in
the giving that we can ever become.

-Jessie Garber

... embers

each night, i wrap my heart's
hope in lace to preserve its embers
from earthly gusts, fill my shelves
with paper treasure and my eyes with
the emphatic *[so m e th i ng]* i search for
in those-that-meet-mine on damp city
streets, but sometimes i miss the b l o o m
sometimes *i fail, i fail, i falter* and must pluck
dead flowers from the dirt—and though i
s i g h, i offer these tired petals in the letters i
write, and the little lights 'round-my-window,
they *b u z z* to my ear(like tiny fireflies they
whisper)a call to persevere . . .

> *oh, you can, you can, you must*
> attract what you b e c o m e.

-Jessie Garber

... splattered

what does it mean to be
a good person?
i think i am still learning
but i do know that my love
is the greatest power i have
my soul a cup of shimmering
gold liquid i strive to keep full
so that i may *pour pour pour*
a bit into this world each day
i have seen it change others
making them more *them-like* and
i have seen it change me too
but i think i am not done
with this *loving-myself-thing*
just yet and i don't think i
want to see a day that
i am not splattered in gold
from *trying* and *spilling*
and t r y i n g again.

-Jessie Garber

... lather

lather me in umellow yellow
i live in my own constellation
create my own magic wonders
where sunlight is liquid hope
sinking warm into these bones
drinking in visions of wide-open fields
i am running wildly through
unmarred by depth or worry or fear
running past the thousands of lives
i could have lead with even one
simple-changed nod of the head
but i chose to jump, to leave, to be
in awe of, honoring, my choice
to be f r e e.

-Jessie Garber

... i am

i am the warm crackling
of needle laying on record.
the music you hum without realizing.
i am soft embers fueling powerful
flames, dark chocolate melting
in your mouth. i am the sun hitting
your cheek after years of shade. i am
close-eyed laughter in the rain, the barefoot
pursuit of lightning, the spontaneous
hands-held dance in the dark. i am the
exuberant scream echoing from the
mountaintops, the leap from fourteen-
thousand feet. i am your golden dream upon
the hill. i am eyes that can collapse stone and
command oceans. a will that dispels fear
and shatters hate into shards—a glass crown
for the invincible. i am the confidence to
speak, and the resolve to do what you say
you will do. to be who you are. limitless, bright,
boundless. i am the greatest adventure, and as
i have always been, i will always be.
p o t e n t / pu r po se ful / and
whole - heart ed ly
me.

-Jessie Garber

... whol–ly

there are days
where my skin glows gold
and i am a magnet, smiling at
strangers and attracting the good,
capturing only light in my wake.
days where the mundane becomes
a holy ritual; i paint my lips red and
dabble the apples of my cheeks in coral,
thanking mother nature for the extra
ounces of soft skin that trace my arms
and grace my stomach.

i love you, i love you.
the world knows it's true,
but i was glowing,
i was warmth,
i was a sight to behold . . .

i was whole, and i was holy.
long before. i met you.

-Jessie Garber

... *blooms*

if i could live in
your eyes when they smile,
i would
for they live in
seasides and
evergreens, in
every mountain peak
i have ever seen
—and in the way i feel
when i see a child laugh
and hope ours will be
just like you

if i could live in your eyes,
i would
because everything
inside of them
(that blooms when you smile)
has forever lived
in me too.

-Jessie Garber

... hallowed

i met you and knew
no one could ever love you
the way that i do(the way you were
meant to be, my *d e a r*)
i did not need to study
your whys and becauses;
it was the only language
that ever
came naturally
to me

on hallowed tongue
we spoke only
in whens(*never* hows)
and fortune came home
for it knew that
even if trees
were purple and flowers
orange(like the glow from your
mind when you
tell me your dreams)that
you and i would still meet to
discuss these things
       and you'd smile
       and i'd smile
       and.
       we'd. know.

what it means.

-Jessie Garber

... *viscous*

what is the opposite
of longing,   the rolled-sleeve
relax once pining dissipates

the reverent empty of
mind where thoughts slow-
burn as stars fade on
fainting cosmic crumbs

i watch the world spin
dizzying pirouettes of time
devotion
loss and
memory

'til eyes blossom flowers
and moments make a fool
of my
aspirations

your angel-aura stops the
twirling, begs for viscosity,
pours that *run run run*
but never drip

and, for you(only for you)
        i can. and i will.

-Jessie Garber

... the weight of us

i love you in heaping quantums
stark contrast to the humble strong of your hand
softly gripping the watering can, tipping into plants
peering over with ardent eyes for hopeful growth

i see it in the mass of white nothingness that is
thick and lightly dense like daylight pouring onto the
hardwood in our empty house, blinding me as we climb
stairs that creak an old chorus to the weight of us

i believe in this, the gritty core of the in-betweens
the moments before we get the things we've dreamed
this calloused tough of you and me and our sticky-sweet
something that has made my heart sing.

-Jessie Garber

... celestial

i dream of being airy as
cosmic dust, so insignificant
that even the littlest things
wield significance. i dream of the
redwoods and the way their
branches hold the sun and drip
the rain. i dream of dissolving
into the grass; into deep forest
green, everlast. of staring up the
steep mountainside—rocks carved by
drifting waves and incessant tide. of
sprawling, spanning sapphire things
and holding stars like diamond rings.
i dream, i dream, of you and me, and
how i'd lay the planets down at your feet.
how i'd relinquish all that's bleak and
dire just to hear the singing of the celestial
choir. but more than that, when fear
grips and mires, i dream of a heart,
of a hope, that beats and beats, but
          n e v e r.   t i r e s.

-Jessie Garber

... the metronome

submerged—i emerge;
soaking and sleepy-eyed.
aimlessly, i look up at the
skyscrapers that wink
at me as i walk, a silent
metronome to drown the
sounds of traffic. the wind
still whistles from the balconies
and light still leaps from the
trees. my cheeks are rosy
and warm, barely containing a
feverish love that refuses to quit.

-Jessie Garber

... *fervently*

spring has a hold on me
a gallant grip reeling under the
guise of a crystalline daydream

where morning breeze devours the day
before sweetly spitting sunshine onto the
fallen petals that lie, disgraced in the grass

why the shame, floral shaves? to fall first
is to fall without fear; to fall fervently
is but a feverish dream(some would say,
an act of h o p e)

i would surely prefer to fly down
                              down
                    down
than simply stare at the ground with
mere fantasies of just-how-soft the
emerald grass could sound.

-Jessie Garber

... bonfire

i have arrived. i feel this
life is finally in full flame.
dancing shades of atomic
tangerine and carmine,
after years of what i learned
to be intentionally fruitless
spark. i like to believe the fire was
a bit of luck—a charmed blink
of the universe, but what i do know
is that the whole time, i was striking
the sticks i chose for myself
and i did not stop. i did not waver
through the friction until
there was smoke; until my life
was gloriously ablaze

—and now i am burning in the very best way

-Jessie Garber

... bone and vein

this elation is scot-free.
like if you turned me inside-out, my blood
would shimmer. i am all bone and vein. cut
to the core. a laser-trimmed paper dream
—only the best words have been scrawled
on me. i have saved them for the world,
to bury in the dirt and sing through
the trees. unbutton these past lives;
n o t h i n g burdens me. i am glowing in
the dark, ready to b e. ready to
burst. i am
confetti
at the
seams.

-Jessie Garber

Fahmida

@fahmidapoetry

Fahmida is an Artist and Author of a poetry book "Maroon Dreams" from India. Her poetries and illustrations have been published in an anthology called "Asian Voices" in U.K 2019 and "Instapoet" - a collection of best poets on Instagram by Augie's Bookshelf. Writing poetries is her dream job and being fond of nature, she wants to travel widely around the world exploring places. You can find traces of nature in her poetry. She recently began sharing her poetry publicly via social media. She says: "poetry to me is what water is to fish." Besides writing, she also enjoys painting, crafting and gardening. You can find her socially on Instagram at : @fahmidapoetry

... *know your worth*

you are struggling, you are battling with
your own self. this immense pain you are in
is meant to leave soon. let the waves of emotions
pour out. let the pain escape. your spines
was never meant to carry them.
you make yourself look like
wrecked street in curfew-imposed city?
but you should know your worth.
your heart is a temple, and the only
pilgrims with pure intentions could enter it.
you have fields of sunflowers on your skin
blooming out of every cracks and crevices,
ready to be harvest and the next batch
to come and so on.
how could you think of giving up?
when the sun and the moon and all the rains
have encircled you to grow wildly.
my dear you were created out of universe.
the galaxies rest on your lashes and stardust
sprinkled on your hair and your body has the
glimmer of the moon.
how could you not shine?
you are anything and everything you
ever wanted to be. let yourself shine like a star.

-Fahmida

... don't be afraid

Let the cascade of memories flow.
Perhaps, remembrance is what
they are made for.
Don't be afraid of dark.
Let it come,
but don't let it settle down.
For you is not a home
for darkness, but a garden
whose flowers are ready to bloom
even in the dark.
So you see,
your dark is not dark,
but an invitation for light
to come in and germinate
the dormant seeds of hope.

-Fahmida

... just a little longer

Ignore what their mouths spit,
just follow your dreams
and you'll be invincible.
Trust me the courage you need
to stand again
in the light is coming
your way.
Just hold on a little longer.

-Fahmida

... *sword of justice*

When the smoke of fear
grip the kingdom,
and the terror prevails
over the people of innocence.
When the scale bodied giant
creature spitting fire
in a human skin
threatens the kingdom.
Then stands a brave
~~prince~~ princess with her
sword of justice.

-Fahmida

... you are the power

When your nightmares come mocking
and you can't think of anything.
When you feel like your heart has been
shattered into minute particles,
and your fear comes creeping in.
Remember who you are
and what you are capable of.
It's time to scuff off the past that has been
haunting you for so long.
The creased pages of your book tells
the stories of abuse, harassment and inequality.
Do we really deserve that?
No!
Now is the time to wash away the rust
your tears have created in your soul.
It's time to change.
Time to fight back for what's right.
It's time to stand.
It's time to find my escape,
your escape.
For you are a woman,
And they shouldn't dare awake
the wolf inside of you.

-Fahmida

... points you should remember while starting your day

--- Draw your curtains and let the sun rays
    kiss your skin gently.
--- Look in the mirror and smile at the
    beautiful soul looking back at you.
--- Gift yourself a flower.
--- You are doing great, just keep on
    doing and moving.
--- Be kind to yourself.
--- Be thankful for what you have and
    and what you don't.

-Fahmida

... give yourself a break

Give yourself a break,
give rest to your body.
Even if you sacrifice
every inch of it,
they will say.

"you weren't good enough."

so girl.
Give yourself a break.

-Fahmida

... the girl of wild

It is in your eyes,
the light which will never
go off you.
The spark that produces
when you touch is enough
to burn the whole forest down.
You carry embers
beneath your tongue,
and wear grace on the curve
of your upper lips.
You are *the girl of wild*
with a chest inhaling rage
and exhaling fire.

-Fahmida

... existence

You can't deny your existence.
You are born to do great things
and not just sob for things
happened to you.
Past can never change,
but future is up to you.
So think about it when
you doubt your existence
once
twice
thrice.
And never repeat the sentence,
"Why did it happened to me."
Blade out past and move ahead.

-Fahmida

... *worth*

You are terrifyingly capable
of what you think you can not.
So stop wasting time on thinking
that you are anything less.
You are the creation of this universe.
And how miraculous is that?

-Fahmida

... *part beautiful part ugly*

The beautiful part is
we humans have got this life to
share,
care,
to love and
to be loved.
To know your purpose,
for what you've been created
and cherish your precious dreams.
But the ugly truth is we have
taken this life for granted.

-Fahmida

... she is the carrier

Tell her nothing about
heartbreaks and hope.

She has been carrying
it since long ago.

-Fahmida

... lesson

Under the magical stack
of sunless sky,
resting upon the line alone.
With every stride of wind
touching her strength,
she closed her eyes
hoping better in the
mirror of tomorrow.

-Sparrow

-Fahmida

... we are the same

It's not about the religion.
It's not about the race.
The blood runs the same
red colour in our veins.
This dividing inequality
is insane.
Stealing our rights,
fading lights
will no longer
be faded.
Tomorrow comes with the
hope of new day,
a better day
a good day.
With love in our hearts
and kindness in our hands,
whatever comes we will
firmly stand.

-Fahmida

... ocean

In an amniotic ocean
what called supreme of the nature.
A soul resuscitates an untold
birth of innocence.
Unwinding the helix of
unrevealed mysteries it holds.
The saviour of being.
Let the pain immerse in waves.
Let the salt heal the wounds
Of primordial aches of lives.

-Fahmida

... rain

The grey sky rips itself apart,
letting rain drops fall on the earth.
Pure enough to wash away the dirt
we have showcased in ourselves.
Let's just stand in the rain,
where sins are forgiven and new
chances awaits.
Where flowers grow and
seed germinate deep
roots in the soil of hope.
Dancing to the beat of thunder
purify your rusted soul.
Fall and stand and fall again.
But don't let the stain remain
Let the rain heals
the wounds old and new.
Let it catch your falling tears
and dissolved it
like it never existed.
Breathe again, the world beneath
your feet is ready to begin.

-Fahmida

... i will rise

I was betrayed
I was wronged
Every time I raised my voice.
Numb and silenced,
that's what they did best to me.
But even with my wings cut
And back stabbed.
My claws they ignored;
and all I did was crawl
crawl and crawl.
These wounds will heal,
these tears will nourish
my bruised heart
and one day my barren land
will grow the fields of flowers
beneath the golden glorious sun.
I will shine a light of hope and equality.
And all the silenced voices
will rise again with a
hope of new beginning.
After dawn a new day.

-Fahmida

... healing is within

All these time, I've learned
the beauty of breaking gracefully.
I've learned the art of healing,
And I happened to know that
it is within, and not anywhere else.
So why not just be a complete
package and stop searching things
where they do not belong?

-Fahmida

... i'm me!

Yes,
I'm me not her,
She's her not me.

I stand my place,
she stands her.

She could never be me,
I could never be her.

Comparing.

That's what you did,
but know that I'll always be myself
and I would never change.
My flaws are mine
my beauty is divine.
And I would never ever
compare me with her and
she could never ever be like me.

-Fahmida

... *fearless*

I've spent too much time of
my life thinking
what if, why, should I ?
How fool I was to think all of that,
or maybe still.
But now I'm building an institution
within me of courage concrete,
ceiling bother proof and windows
of confidence that only sieve
tremendous positive light
enough to grow my inner strength
and know my capabilities.
That I'm ready to spread my wings
without a second thought and
fly fearlessly.

-*Fahmida*

... girl! know who you really are

I'm the thousand wind blowing across
the sea over the mountains.
I'm the pouring rain gentle enough
to nurture seeds to grow.
I'm the thunderclap in the dark deep
clouds growling miles away.

You haven't even known the
slightest of me.
Don't you ever dare judge me,
underestimate me.
Don't you ever dare awake
the wolf inside of me.

I'm not a girl with a glass heart
that you could shatter it easily,
but a hurricane wrapped
in bloody walls that won't
hesitate destroying things.

-Fahmida

... claws

Clipping her wings
won't stop her from
doing what she loves.

You clipped and forgot
she has claws.

-Fahmida

... dream

Last night I dreamt of me
swimming swiftly in
ocean's waves.
Cuddling baby dolphins
In my embrace.
Sky deep blue lit with stars –

a beautiful flickering assemblage.

Floating on water
with my hands and
feet stretched,
I stared the enchanting
sky and counted
shooting stars like

1....2....3....

And in that moment I was
completely free in the vast
ocean of my dreams.

-Fahmida

... women are like that

Women are like that,
magic flows in their veins.
Starlight shimmers in their eyes.
Music flows when they walk.
They wear a skin like soft petals
And their heart made of gold.

-Fahmida

... the giver

Dig all of it,
every single fibre of
Love,
Care and
Hope
from your heart
as pure as gold.

Some of which
you can give them
to those,
who need them most.

-Fahmida

Phoebe Tee

@phoebeelicious

Phoebe is a native from the Philippines. She is a girl who loves music, art, coffee and books. Reading has not only been a hobby but a saving grace for her. She has always been young at heart despite of all the craziness life threw at her. She remained strong and that's when writing came in. At one of the darkest moments of her life, writing was one that saved her. It was something that helped her push through and took her mind away from the darkness that surrounded her. She used to only write to be a part of their school paper then stopped for about 9 years. Now, for almost 2 years, she started writing again and this time sharing her story through paper and pen. She started sharing her story to the world through her IG poetry page. Writing about her struggles, defeat, scars and victory. She is currently working on her 1st poetry book entitled "SHE" where her untold story awaits to unfold. A book that she hopes to inspire and breathe life to those who have been lost for awhile.

... key

She
Struggled to find her lost self
Leaving her dusty on that empty shelf
It was too dark for her to see
That she herself is the only key

(Key to the door of her mystery
Key to find her finally)

-Phoebe Tee

... stop

She
Had to stop
Stop wallowing in self pity
And start loving herself completely
Because she only has herself to survive
A world that's nothing but evil and bad vibe

-Phoebe Tee

... acceptance

She
Embraced herself for what she truly is
For all her negativity, insecurity
and everything on her list

(She learned to accept herself, flaws and all)

-Phoebe Tee

... wall

She
Thought she was too weak to survive it all
But realized she is more than just a brick on the wall

She is the wall itself
Strong, Sturdy, Hard and never easy to fall

-Phoebe Tee

... live

She
Allowed herself to rise from the dead
Realizing it's time she makes her own bed
To live the life she dreams of living
To redeem herself from constantly dying

(It's time to be FREE)

-Phoebe Tee

... reborn

She
Realized she shouldn't keep watering a dying plant
She has to start anew
Plant a little hope
Wait until it stems
Then grow bloom into the beautiful wild flower
And gain back her lost power

(She's reborn)

-Phoebe Tee

... winner

She
Is a sinner
A dark dangerous sinner
But even that didn't stop her to be a winner
She continues to win against her inner sins
And that my love is where her life truly begins

(Winning against her darkness)

-Phoebe Tee

... fly

She
Discovered the wind to be too comforting
So she jumped from the peak of all
Her misery and fears
Feeling the air kiss her cheek
Finally tasting the freedom
She's been trying to seek

She
Overcame her fear of height
Realizing she deserves to be up there
Shining bright like the stars in the night

-Phoebe Tee

135

... self-love

She
Knew she was too different from the people around her
She was called weird for being better than the other
She tried fitting in just to be accepted
Then realized she didn't have to fit in to be wanted
She needs to acknowledge and appreciate herself that she
took for granted

(Love yourself more when others can't love you)

-Phoebe Tee

... galaxy

She
Allowed the stars to shine in her eyes
Allowed the moon to take away her disguise
Showing the world she's an entire galaxy
Of everything that she's meant to be

(Planet and stars sprouted from her scars)

-Phoebe Tee

... diamond

She
Is a diamond in the rough
Rare and pure made to be tough
Beware of her beautiful yet sharp edges though
She's won and championed all her battles in a row

-Phoebe Tee

... warrior

She
Is a constant contradiction of darkness and light
But she is a warrior who chose to live and continued to
fight

-Phoebe Tee

... imperfect

She
Is not perfect
So far from it in all honesty
She could be strong as you
But breaks down too
She could be smiling wide
And yet her pains she still hides inside
She is covered in battle scars from her victories
But is still hunted by her dark memories

She is a work in progress
But is gorgeously trying nevertheless

-Phoebe Tee

... hot and cold

She
Is fire and ice
Hot and cold
She might confuse you with everything that she holds
But damn it if she's not the finest piece of Gold

(She is a mixture of both but priceless nevertheless)

-Phoebe Tee

... happy

She
Spilled bright colorful hues
On her sad emotional blues
And cured her sadness
With every doze of happiness
That she could find within
Mending the darkness
That lives under her skin

(Because now, she's choosing to be happy)

-Phoebe Tee

... bloom

She
Allowed flowers to bloom through her scars
Showing the world she's more than
Those nasty marks

She
Allowed light to come in
To seep into the depths of her skin
To warm her deep inside
Allowing life to revive everything that has died

-Phoebe Tee

... no

She
Grew amongst all the wild flowers in the meadow
She rose above everyone who told her NO

-Phoebe Tee

... hero

She
Has always been her own protector
Always fought like a warrior
She started from scratch
From zero
Now she is her very own hero

-Phoebe Tee

... alive

She
Finally felt at peace within
Letting sunlight and rainbow
Seep through her skin
She is no longer dull and black
Colors filled her and everything she lack

(She felt alive)

-Phoebe Tee

...home

She
Has gone far and wide
Looking for someplace
She could finally call home
Not knowing
She is home all along
That to herself is where
She truly belong

She is her only destiny
That after all the time of searching and hurting
She found herself finally!

-Phoebe Tee

...anew

She
Built herself with the confidence of a warrior
Who has been through all horror
This time she's no longer scared to push through
To the challenges of life as she starts anew

-Phoebe Tee

... rise

She
Is purity in its perfect form
Too confident to conform to the society's fake norm
She walked through fire and burned in hell
Buried herself in an endless well
Only to rise once more
And be stronger than before

-Phoebe Tee

... sing

She
Sang her heart out
Telling the world her story and what's it about
She allowed her voice to penetrate souls
Patching what's broken and covering wholes

(She healed herself and then maybe some)

-Phoebe Tee

... finally

She
Kept on singing
Until her heart is no longer hurting
Until her heart begins beating
Until all she could hear is
The angelic sound of her inner melody
Discovering her lost voice finally

(She's back)

-Phoebe Tee

... enough

She
Realized that she didn't need anybody's opinion
To tell her and convince her that she is beautiful and
worth it
For she knew it deep within her
And that is most definitely enough
Ma'am and Sir

(Look inside you, it's there)

-Phoebe Tee

... art

She
Is a force to be reckoned with
Fought her battles
Won her wars
Wore her scars like fine pieces of arts

-Phoebe Tee

... queen

She
Is the strongest woman I have ever seen
Truly a Brave
Respectable
Undefeated Queen

-Phoebe Tee

... just like you

She
Was once just like you
Naïve
Broken
Scared
Insecure
Lost

But she pushed through
She hopes you do too

(Please don't give up on yourself)

-Phoebe Tee

Sky Rose Heywood

@skyrosepoetess

Sky Rose Heywood is a mother, poet, author, youtuber, creatrix and entrepreneur. She lives in the UK with her partner and their three children. Her writing is a blend of spirituality, nature, equality and empowerment, with a dash of fantasy and magick. Author of the Foxglove and Rose Poetry Collection, which explores violence against women and healing after abuse, self-love and empowerment.

... lilith

Lilith is with me
As I step towards the future
Rising and rewilding my mind
I join the ranks
Of this fight
Feel the fierce flame
Of divine feminine
Burst through my chants
As I give thanks
To my Goddess Lilith
For giving me the strength
To stand in my power
Hour after hour
To never break or bend
To the will of them
Hail the dark goddess
For the beacons are lit
Women calling for aid
And the battle cry of women
Shall roll across the land
As our feet stamp the streets
Fighting the system
That wants to demonise women
So demons we shall become
With horned crowns
And strong hearts
Demon Queens are we
Lilith is with me
And every women
As we march into our power

-Sky Rose Heywood

... toxic web

Caught in this toxic web
Web of life and death and nothingness
Nothingness licking our wounds
Wounds wound round the web
Web strengthened by those wounds
Wounds festering and pilfering life
Life lost in this web of sickening
Sickening sounds slipping into souls
Souls burnt and singed for too many years
Years and years we have fought
Fought to be released from these threads
Threads tangled and tight
Tight around chests, squeeze the breath
Breath beaten and blackened by burnt bones
Bones of these old souls, in young torment
Torment of tight rope trips
Trips around the weavers threads
Threads connecting us all to toxicity
Toxicity dampening our lives, dumbing
Dumbing us down until we don't question
Question it, question it now
Now rise up together, scream and break
Break the bonds of this toxic web

-Sky Rose Heywood

... skin

Every month we change our skin
Every month I would wish for a tougher one
Every month I would be dismayed
Finding it's just as soft

How could I make it tougher?
Toughen up, grow a thicker skin!
You must have a stiff upper lip!
Be a strong woman!

Every month I failed.
My skin was soft, gentle and barely covered my heart
Seen as weak
But try as I might, I couldn't change my DNA

Now I realise I am perfect
And my strength is in my weakness
My compassion is strength
Now I accept this skin I am in

-Sky Rose Heywood

... where?

Where is the panacea for this dystopia
Where is the answer, to these hollow questions
How can we change to a semblance of utopia
How can we fit to the lightened muse

How can we see with stone eyes
Wind changes fast, time changes slow
Where is the magic 8 ball to show us lies
Where are the answers to life's deep queries

Where is the love, in a world moulded forlorn
Where is the equality, in a world of difference
Where is the calm, in this world of storm
Where is the lightened muse when needed

How can we grow as a populace
When our fires are doused, held down
Stunted growth, snails pace
We need to fast forward

Where is the magic looking glass
We can dive through to a new world
To a better world, start a new class
Growing with love and clarity

-Sky Rose Heywood

... something

There was something in her eyes that night
Something that sizzled, something that stirred
Something that rattled cages and bones
Something that screamed at my silence
Something that squeezed my stifled soul
Something that dove between my shoulder blades, ripping
through my whipped skin and ruffling my long forgotten
feathers

There was something in her eyes that night
Something that erased the illusion
Something that woke me up
Something that spoke in languages long forgotton
Something that scared me, excited and ignited me
Something that made me stand for the first time in my
life with my eyes pinned open, knowing they would
never close again on reality

There was something in her eyes that started our
revolution.

-Sky Rose Heywood

... weeds

Weeds are we, common as muck
Spreading our seeded serenades all over
Singing joyous rebellion for the masses
These seeds planted years ago
By ancestors forgotten
Seeds flew on ensanguined zephyr
To thrive new minds
To open the masses rose coloured eyes
With thistle and prickles and sharp truths to cut
Cut the ground walked upon
To breathe in the freedom of light

-Sky Rose Heywood

... when women rise

Years of tears and fears
Breathed collectively
Through torment
In blood drenched hands
We are still hurting
Still stifled
Still controlled
Still sliced and broken
Still pulled
Still repairing our hearts (cuts)
Still waiting
Still demanding
Still protesting

When women rise together
We can entomb inequality
Lay it down to rest
Buried deep
Never to resurface again

When women rise
We can show how strong we are
We can breathe life into this dying ember
We can black boot and red lip
We can baggy t shirt and cap
We can power suit and heel
Never to kneel again
No bloody knees for them

When women rise
We can lift the weight of hindered hearts
We can buff and shine rusty halos
We can singe the word consent into the minds of all
We can scour the world for wounded
We can nurture and care
We can change the paradigm
When women rise

-Sky Rose Heywood

... it's time

Now it's time to stand up for women's rights
Speak up, let our voice remove the taboo
The insidious secrets – we must fight

With many women hurting out of sight
We must shine a light, search for hidden clue
Now it's time to stand up for women's rights

Offer support, empathy for their plight
Leave victim blaming, no help will it do
The insidious secrets - we must fight

Many women kept silent in affright
With harrowing statistics, a preview
Now it's time to stand up for women's rights

Greatly needed - society rewrite
A wall of strength, violence will not break through
The insidious secrets - we must fight

Believing we can shift cynical sight
Be a people, survivors can turn to
Now it's time to stand up for women's rights
The insidious secrets - we must fight

-Sky Rose Heywood

... *reborn*

We were kindred tombs
Bound together by wombs
Shells forgotten but unforgiven
Lives tainted, sacrifices given
Captive bodies, but free minds
We broke through chains and binds
Free at last from the torment
Of whips and lashing torrent
Of a life split between three
Twisting our souls between thee

Maiden, Mother, Crone
Spoke to us through bone
Interrupting the susurrous slips
With tumultuous tight rope trips
Weaving through our catapulted minds
Free, but still caught in the gear grinds

Laid to rest in the land of taunts
Cradled in the arms of riverbed haunts
Laid to rest but the fight is not over
For we are readying for our final takeover
To be reborn, warrior spirits to the core
Fighting spirits we are, now and forevermore

-Sky Rose Heywood

... to the daughters of millennials

We were called the snowflake generation
But what that means is that we spoke up
We took offence to things that for too long had been
watered down or played off as jokes
We were the nasty women, the angry women
We were then generation of elevation
Rising spiritually, financially and morally
We were the generation of gentle parenting, veganism,
gay marriage legalisation, speaking up for climate change
We were the age of social and it connected us,
empowered us, helped us grow and evolve.

I hope you had a childhood you don't have to heal from

I hope we raised our sons to treat women as equal

I hope that when a man's gaze holds
On the length of your skirt you can
Stare him down, until he shrinks away

I hope that when you are told you can't
You prove to the world that you can and will

I hope that if someone hurts you
Appropriate and fair justice is served

I hope that you never have the words
Slut, bitch, whore thrown at you for simply existing

I hope you can walk home alone without feeling the fear
of rape or assault

I hope all feminism is intersectional and everyone is
respected and their voices heard

I hope there is no need for domestic violence shelters

I hope women locker room jokes have subsided

I hope women aren't objectified to sell products

I hope we have all seen beyond the beauty industry bullshit

I hope all bodies, no matter the size, shape, colour or ability are celebrated and diversity is welcomed

I hope women can have hair under their arms and be accepted

I hope that you can choose your colours, toys, like and dislikes without being forced to like pink, dolls, and pretty dresses

I hope you can talk openly about your periods regardless of who you are around

I hope you are allowed to enter every sacred temple and holy place in this world

I hope there has been a woman president in every country

I hope women take up equal space in positions of power

I hope you are free to marry whomever you wish, or to not marry at all, wherever you live in the world

I hope girls and women are really heard

I hope violence against women and girls has ceased

I hope you feel you can and should take up space in this world

I hope you have autonomy of your body
In every way possible

I hope that virginity isn't still on that fucking pedestal

I hope that you can love and live freely wherever you wish

I hope your faith doesn't minimise your existence

I hope more than anything that you can be seen, heard and valued

I hope you are treated with the respect you deserve

It might take more than our generation to fix this mess
But I hope we have continued from our ancestors
To lay solid foundations for you to continue the fight
You might need to be the snowflake generation 2.0
Because it takes many snowflakes to create an avalanche.

-Sky Rose Heywood

... destroying moulds

We see ourselves through broken eyes
Blinded by the culture, and their lies
Feeding us failure and fat shaming
Holding us up against "perfect framing"

While we gaze into our framed reflection
Sinking us down in diet culture dejection
Contorting our views, to fit the perfect mould
So we continue to despise the curves we hold

Stop trying to fit into that mould
It wasn't made for you to try to fold
Yourself into and pick and pluck
To squeeze and stifle, getting stuck

They don't see your sacrifice or prayer
They don't feel your shame and despair
Those mould makers, sitting up high
Profiting off this wide spread lie

No mould can contain the shape of you
So release the pressure, begin anew
A new time and a mould-less paradigm
Where we can each be ourselves and truly shine

-Sky Rose Heywood

... the woman who

I used to be the woman who was obsessed
Obsessed with trying to impress
Obsessed with the scales
Obsessed with fabricated weight loss tales
Obsessed with colossal calorific deficits
Obsessed with the promised benefits

Until I found self love and was freed
A work in progress, but I planted the seed
I have a lifetime of messages, and conditioning
To unpack, and re-evaluate, mind repositioning
But this growing community is positive
Full of love, strength, fully supportive

That support is essential to survive
In the face of the fake, filtered and Photoshopped lives
The bullies fuelled by hate and brainwashing
They won't stop body shaming and white washing
Making any body that isn't today's beauty pedestal
Feel less than, unworthy and completely unbearable

Their merciless eyes seeking only perfection
Anything less than is met with rejection
Forced by diet culture to have pristine appearance
Anything less than is cursed into disappearance
When 90 percent of us are "less than"
I think it's about time that we banned
These dangerous ideals, make a new plan

-Sky Rose Heywood

... *happily ever after*

A woman I am, a warrior true
Fighting for the chance to be accepted
As love's dying wish searching for a fighter's kiss
Gender doesn't rule our right to be happy
Gender doesn't dictate our autonomy
I beseech you, hear me now

Raise our voices to be heard hereinafter
Raise our children to be their true selves
Not to be afraid to speak their mind ever
Never to accept hurtful types of love
To chase their passions, to be truly happy
To not feel pressured into their first kiss

Let's raise our vision beyond true loves kiss
Fairytale damsels in distress, happily everafter
Let's show strong genders, real life
Not fiction perfection, real, raw and true
Brave pioneers of their field, not sacrificing for love
Let's switch up the fairytales forever

Light up patriarchal shadows
However we can, in the softness of a kiss
Or the recognition of all types of love
The acceptance of diversity hereafter
Showing people, they should all have rights
Affirming that everyone deserves to be happy

No more living in fear, being unhappy
No more denying reality, to fit in however we can
No more sitting in silence, speak up now
Freedom to live, happily ever after
Safe in our identities, safe in our loves

So we will rise and fight together, for love
For freedom, for rights and equality, to be happy
We will smash the walls and build up after
A new land of acceptance, free forever
Free to feel joy in that public kiss
Free to live a life that's true

Inclusive, accepting true loves kiss,
However that looks, love is pure
We all deserve to live happy ever after

-Sky Rose Heywood

... *bring to me*

Bring to me your worries and strife
Release the weight of sorrow
Let go of the pain from trauma
Release the anger within
Let go of the hate in your heart

Bring to me you troubles and sins
Release those high expectations
Let go of the need to please
Release the guilt of self love
Let go of the suffering of life

Place them all in iron this night
Bring them to me
Leaving not a trace within you
Bring them to me
Place them at my feet

One by one we will burn those fears
That anguish
That pain and strife
That guilt and suffering

One by one we will set ablaze
The sins of your lineage
The pain in your heart

We burn these into the longest night
So that you
Dear soul
Can fly from your ashes of anguish
In to a lighter life of love

-Sky Rose Heywood

...singed rose

With broken chords she sang silence
Falling upon deaf ears, this rose sang
Bittersweet darkness dripped from petals
And decay flowed from veins

Using pyromancy, sunken rose whispered
Secrets only the deities could know
For her voice had broken wings and torn petals
Her raven blush was too dark for eyes of sun

Just a gasp of air did leave her lips
As she slowly rose above the shade
Freedom cracked her bones
Gold repaired her and she left

With dignity to guide and wisdom from above
She tracked down her sound, at last she sang proud
A voice lost for yore of sin, now she swam in its din
She sang sweetly of love and lyre, as she rebirthed in fire

-Sky Rose Heywood

... the self love sonnet

The need of sustenance is obvious
Pray tell what fuels our body, mind and soul
We are told, resist the urge to feel whole
Follow blindly, trust us delirious
Eat pure, no carbs, low fat, not perilous
Workout, eat less to gain your body goal
Always be motivated, no cajole
Waning of hope would be disastrous

What if we trusted our bodies to heal
Allowed ourselves to be content as is
Farewell to scales, adios measurements
Within we look, discover how we feel
Define ourselves, provide a new thesis
Self love is crafting brave new insurgents

-Sky Rose Heywood

... worship

Worship your body
As you walk this life
Never bend the knee
To him or them or any hierarchy

You are the goddess
Bow to no deity
Bring your awareness
Within you, not above

You are divinity
Shining bright and true
Your soul is mighty
Holy and sacred you

Rise and stand strong
Let no doubt enter here
Your soul is never wrong
Listen with a loving ear

Worship the feet
That walk your path
Alone you will meet
No heaven bound wrath

For you are true divinity
Everlasting and pure
Embrace your femininity
And never obscure

-Sky Rose Heywood

... waterlily

The Waterlily rose
Even with weeded woes
Clinging to her bare toes
A pure and slow groove she chose

To rise against a dozen obstacles thrown
Using her heartstrings as vines, flown
Out of the regurgitated sandy home
Into the light of day with clear skies shown

The Waterlily flew with the phoenix from destruction
Abound her lay fears of her own execution
From an unrivalled love proclamation
Rippled with seeds of devastating deception

She left it all behind and shone in the shimmer
Indigenous roots began to quiver
As she lay the foundations of a winner
With mirrored streams, clarity aglimmer

-Sky Rose Heywood

... untamed

I am a frozen sun
I am black ice in sight
I am a prim and proper rebel
I sleep between the blankets of snowdrops
And breathe the fire of melted hearts
I am willing wisdom and child's play
I am nonchalant and burnt feeling
I am a candle to warm your life
I am frost climbing your ocean
I am depth of the Mariana
I am reflection of a winter pool
I am the second coming of hope and light
I am darkness of moonless night
I am the enigmatic desire you wish to tame
But I've told you once
Now one last time
I am not bound to this earth
Of dirt and tide anew
I am goddess divine
Who loves you
Make no mistake
I am not one to be tamed
Cease this claim evermore
Or feel the spark of phoenix flame

-Sky Rose Heywood

... potion

Crafting a potion
For every woman
Drink it deep
Let it seep
Stronger and longer
Drink it deep

With the tears of our ancestors
With the roots of a rose
With the forced smiles of women
With the lace of petticoats
With the bones of corsets
With the screams of ages
With the grace of goddesses
With the roars of wombs

Crafting a potion
For every woman
To free us from the trap
Liberate and elevate

With this red tape
Still around our necks
Stifling our words
Silencing our pain
Drink it deep

-Sky Rose Heywood

... call

Conjure your kin
Bring forth your goddess
Call upon wild women
To cast light upon the fallen

May our hearts hold honour
May our gaze be upon the wild
To feel the call within
To reach for each other

Beseech your beauty
Bring forth your goddess
In reverence of truth
In honour of the call

May our truth shine free
May our courage never falter
To bring the fight into light
To bring our revolution

Call forth your covens
Bring forth the goddess
Call upon the wisdom
To bring us to divinity

Hail to the women who rise this night
Hail to the witch, the mother, the crone
Hail to the maiden, the sister, the friend
Hail to the wild women, bleeding and brave

The winds of change, stir across the lands
So awaken the wild women, fierce and free
To bring in a new age, with dignity and light
Wild women, shield maidens, goddesses arise

-Sky Rose Heywood

... love spell

She spent her nights crafting elixirs
Testing her recipe for love
Rainbow filled alchemist vials
Seeking the harbinger of love
Chatoyant crystals adorning her altar
Relentlessly recreating the ritual for love
She was in her prime, oh so ready to bloom
For the efflorescence of love
She craved it, from her darkened room
Her mind, a penumbra of love
She continued, until she mastered the spell
Until a divine connection showed her love
Lightened mind by the lightning bolt
Stuck her heart as she swayed in love
She cooed and sang in dulcet decadence
She had lost it long ago, but found her love
Through the persistence of the powerful
She now swam in gratitude for her self love

-Sky Rose Heywood

... of wings and crowns

Looking deep into the wells of your eyes
Seeing my crown glisten in your tears
Please know that I am here
I hold this space for you, sweet soul
I am love and serenity
Come sit beneath my wings a while
Let me carry your heavy heart
Let me shield your soul
With my divine grace
Stay with me a while and rest
Let me help you create your own crown
Out of the light of your future
The ashes of your past
and the jewels of your present
So when you are ready to rise again
You will rise a Queen
A Goddess, almighty and strong
So you may shelter others under your wings of grace
Together my love, we can bring a unity
A song for all to sing of wings and crowns
Of Goddesses and Queens
But for now, sweet soul
Rest
Rest beneath my wings
You are safe here

-Sky Rose Heywood

... now

I will speak my truth
Through bones of time
For I vanquished the vanity of these veins
I locked in the landscapes of love
Roaming through the valleys and copse
I sought the wolf within and wailed with wild
The wilderness in me awoke, woes wilted
These waves of thought spinning gold
Into my tapestry of time
And now
And from now
For evermore
I evoke
The Goddess of fire
Engulfing the sins
I speak my truth now
No more tight-lipped tightrope trips
I wrestled the wraiths and wrongs
To be born anew
With obsidian to protect me
Moonlit waves in serene mind
Cool, calm and courageous
Yes, now
Now I speak my truth
And all shall hear it

-Sky Rose Heywood

... uncaged

In my opinion the colours of victory
can only be a rainbow
Where everyone of every kind is shown liberty
A convocation of souls united to bestow
The gift of freedom and flame on history

Opening of windows, doors and shores
For everyone is welcome in this new land
Land of peace with new equality laws
Where people come together hand in hand

Bidding adieu to the wrongs of yesteryear
Brave faced and hopeful we stride into new age
No longer bombs blasting living in fear
Raising each other as we raise the bars of oppressive
cage

-Sky Rose Heywood

<u>*Find the Authors*</u>

Iva Markicevic
    Instagram   @sa.te.llights

Sundancer
    Instagram   @sundancer.poetry

M.G.M.
    Instagram   @michelle.nicole.gerrard
    Pinterest   The Vibrant Kitchen & Home
                                 www.pinterest.com/chellemarriott

Nina Green
    Instagram   @nina_green_poetry

Jessie Garber
    Instagram   @cosmic.ramblings

Fahmida
    Instagram   @fahmidapoetry
    Twitter   @backtosunshine

Phoebe Tee
    Instagram   @phoebeelicious

Sky Rose Heywood
    Instagram   @skyrosepoetess